MW00614526

This book belongs to

Name: _____

Cover Design by :
Gowri Vemuri

First Edition :
May, 2019

Third   Edition   :
April , 2021

Author :
Gowri Vemuri

Edited by :
Ritvik Pothapragada

Questions: mathknots.help@gmail.com

NOTE : VDOE is neither affiliated nor sponsors or endorses this product.

Visit www.a4ace.com

Also available more time based practice tests on subscription

This book is dedicated to:

My Mom, who is my best critic, guide and supporter.

To what I am today, and what I am going to become tomorrow,

is all because of your blessings, unconditional affection and support.

This book is dedicated to the

strongest women of my life,

my dearest mom

and

to all those moms in this universe.

G.V.

www.a4ace.com   www.math-knots.com

The Virginia Board of Education and Virginia Department of Education (VDOE) have developed the Virginia Assessment Program (VAP) to measure and evaluate students' academic progress in the Standards of Learning (SOLs). The SOLs indicate Virginia's expectations for what students should know and be able to do in the subject areas of reading, writing, mathematics, science, and history/social science.

Students in grades 3-12 to take the Standards of Learning (SOL) assessments each year. Some of the tests are required by all students each year, and others are required only at specific grade levels. Additionally, with the removal of some SOL tests in recent years, the VDOE assigned the responsibility of the creation and administration of alternate, performance - based assessments on local divisions. Student scores from these tests determine a school's and the division's state accreditation and measures progress toward meeting federal targets.

Virginia Standards of Learning (SOL) tests are generally given online unless a student has an identified and documented need to be assessed using paper,pencil format. The test question format is typically multiple choice, and each test contains some technology enhanced items.

GRADE 3-8 STANDARDS OF LEARNING(SOL) TESTS

GRADE 3	GRADE 4	GRADE 5	GRADE 6	GRADE 7	GRADE 8
	VIRGINIA STUDIES				WRITING
MATH	MATH	MATH	MATH	MATH	MATH
READING	READING	READING	READING	READING	READING
		SCIENCE			SCIENCE

NOTE : VDOE is neither affiliated nor sponsors or endorses this product.

END OF COURSE STANDARDS OF LEARNING (SOL) TESTS

GRADE 9	GRADE 10	GRADE 11
ALGEBRA I	GEOMETRY	ALGEBRA II
EARTH SCIENCE	BIOLOGY	CHEMISTRY
WORLD HISTORY I	WORLD HISTORY II	VIRGINIA & US HSTORY
		WORLD GEOGRAPHY
		ENGLISH : READING
		ENGLISH : WRITING

Any Student taking one of the courses listed here is expected to take the corresponding end-of-course SOL test. The grade levels depicted here represent grade level at which students typically participate in these courses.

NOTE : VDOE is neither affiliated nor sponsors or endorses this product.

SOL Test Scoring and Performance Reports:

Standards of Learning assessments in English reading, mathematics, science and history/social science are made up of 35-50 items or questions that measure content knowledge, scientific and mathematical processes, reasoning and critical thinking skills. English writing skills are measured with a two-part assessment that includes multiple-choice items and an essay.

Student performance is graded on a scale of 0-600 with 400 representing the minimum level of acceptable proficiency and 500 representing advanced proficiency. On English reading and mathematics tests, the Board of Education has defined three levels of student achievement: basic, proficient, and advanced, with basic describing progress towards proficiency.

Performance Achievement Levels:

- The achievement levels for grades 3-8 reading and mathematics tests are: *Pass/Advanced, Pass/Proficient, Fail/Basic,* and *Fail/Below Basic.*

- The achievement levels for science tests, history tests, and End-of-Course (EOC) tests* are: *Pass/Advanced, Pass/Proficient,* and *Fail/Does Not Meet.*

- The EOC Writing (2010 SOL) test, EOC Reading (2010 SOL) test, and EOC Algebra II (2009 SOL) test have an achievement level of *Advanced/College Path* in place of the *Pass/Advanced* achievement level.

NOTE : VDOE is neither affiliated nor sponsors or endorses this product.

INDEX

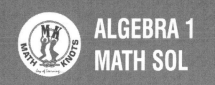
FORMULA SHEET

1. Area of a triangle

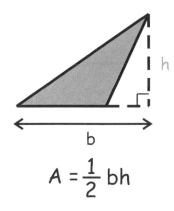

$$A = \frac{1}{2} bh$$

2. Area of a parellelogram

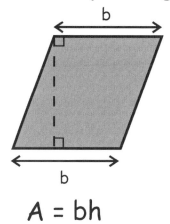

$$A = bh$$

3. Volume and Surface area of a Cuboid

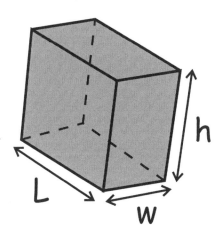

$$V = lwh$$
$$S.A = 2(lw + lh + wh)$$

4. volume and Surface area of a Cone

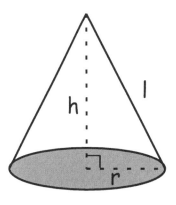

$$V = \frac{1}{3} \Pi r^2$$
$$S.A = \Pi r(l + h)$$

5. Perimeter and Area of a Square

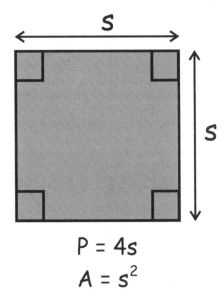

$$P = 4s$$
$$A = s^2$$

6. Area of a Trapezium

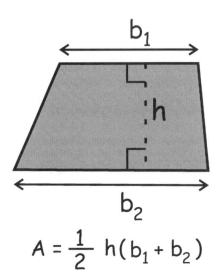

$$A = \frac{1}{2} h(b_1 + b_2)$$

7. Volume and Surface area of a Cylinder

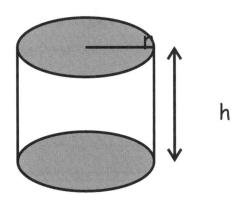

$$V = \Pi r^2 h$$
$$S.A = 2\Pi r(h+r)$$

8. Volume and Surface area of a Pyramid

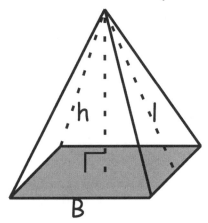

$$V = \frac{1}{3} Bh$$
$$S.A = \frac{1}{2} lp + B$$

www.a4ace.com   www.math-knots.com

9. Circumference and Area of a Circle

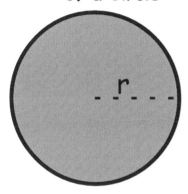

$$c = 2\Pi r$$
$$A = \Pi r^2$$

pi

$$\Pi = 3.14$$
$$\Pi = \frac{22}{7}$$

10. Right angled Triangle (Pythagoran)

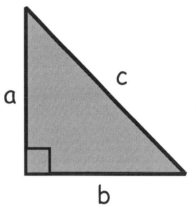

$$c^2 = a^2 + b^2$$

**Pythagorean triplets
Examples** : (3 , 4 , 5)
(5 , 12 , 13)
(7 , 24 , 25)
(15 , 20 , 25)
(6 , 8 , 10)
(9 , 12 , 15)
(6 , 8 , 10)
(12 , 16 , 20)
(10 , 24 , 26)

11. Perimeter and Area of a Rectangle

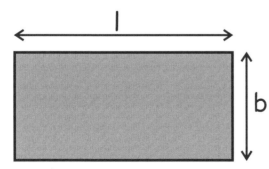

Area = l   b   ×
Perimeter = 2(l + b)

12. Quadratic formula

$$x = \frac{-b \pm \sqrt{b^2 - 4ac}}{2a}$$

13. Algebraic Identities

$$(a + b)^2 = a^2 + 2ab + b^2$$

$$(a - b)^2 = a^2 - 2ab + b^2$$

$$a^2 - b^2 = (a + b) (a - b)$$

$$a^2 + b^2 = (a + b)^2 - 2ab$$

$$a^2 + b^2 = (a - b)^2 + 2ab$$

14. Equation of a Straight line

$y = mx + c$
Where m = slope
c = y - intercept

www.a4ace.com   www.math-knots.com

Abbreviations

milligram	mg	volume	V
gram	g	total Square Area	S.A
kilogram	kg	area of base	B
milliliter	mL	ounce	oz
liter	L	pound	lb
kiloliter	kL	quart	qt
millimeter	mm	gallon	gal.
centimeter	cm	inches	in.
meter	m	foot	ft
kilometer	km	yard	yd
square centimeter	cm^2	mile	mi.
cubic centimeter	cm^3	square inch	sq in.
		square foot	sq ft
year	yr	cubic inch	cu in.
month	mon	cubic foot	cu ft
hour	hr		
minute	min		
second	sec		

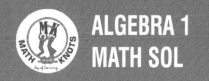

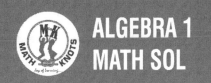

1.   Solve for v from the below equation

$$-3(-6v - 1) = (-4(5 - 4v)) + 1$$

(A) 11   (B) -11   (C) -4   (D) 5

2.   If f(k) = -3k + 1 then which of the below best describes the graph f(k)

(A) Slope =   3,   y-intercept = 2
(B) Slope = - 3,   y-intercept = 1
(C) Slope = - 3,   y-intercept = -1
(D) Slope =   3,   y-intercept = -2

3.   Find the slope of the line in the graph below

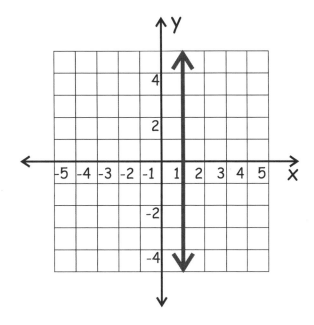

(A)   1   (B)   0   (C)   undefined   (D)   2

4. Which of the below order pair is the solution of the below system of equations ?

$$p - 2q = -18$$
$$2p + q = -6$$

(A) (-6, 6)   (B) (0, 6)   (C) (6, 6)   (D) (6, 0)

5. Solve the following inequality ?

$$204 < -6 (-4m - 2)$$

(A) m > 20   (B) m < -40   (C) m > -21   (D) m > 8

6. The equation of the line 'm' is represented by which of the below options ?

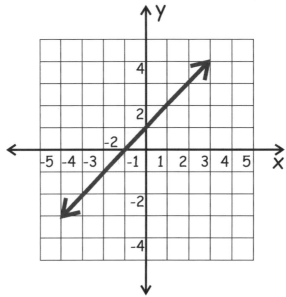

(A) y = -x - 1   (B) y = 2x + 2

(C) y = 3x + 1   (D) y = 2x - 1

7. Which of the below quadratic equation has roots of 10 and -11 ?

   (A) $g^2 - g + 110 = 0$ (B) $g^2 + 21g + 110 = 0$

   (C) $g^2 + g - 110 = 0$ (D) $g^2 + g - 10 = 0$

8. Which graph best represents the equation

$$y = \frac{-9}{4}x + 5$$

(A)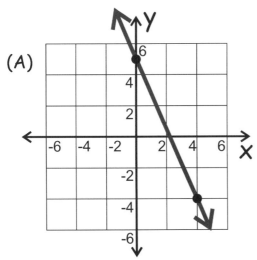

(B)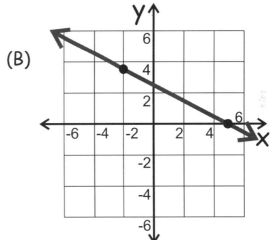

(C)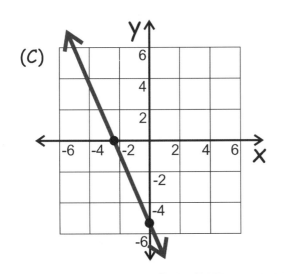

(D)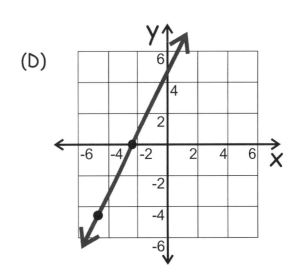

9. System of linear equations are shown in the graph below. Which of the
    below is the solution of the system of linear equations ?

$$y = \frac{7}{8}x - 9$$

$$y = -2$$

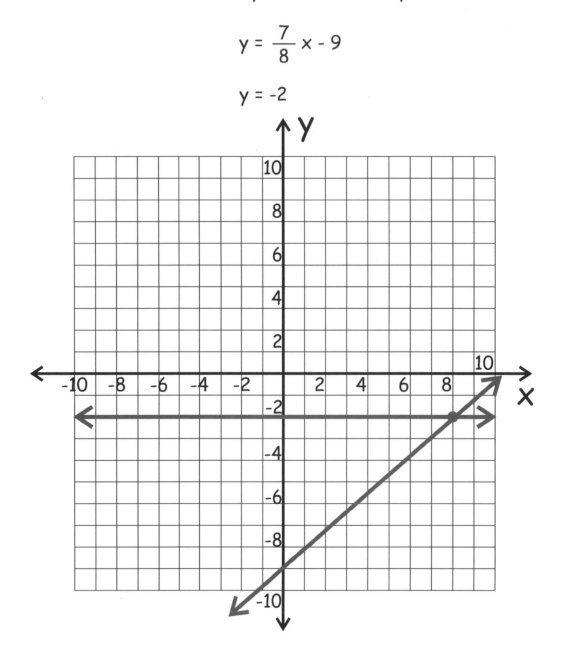

(A) (8 , 5)   (B) (2 , -8)

(C) (8 , -2)   (D) (-2 , 8)

10. Which of the below represents distributive property ?

(A) $6(1 + 9v) = 6 + 54v$

(B) $1 + 5v = 5v + 1$

(C) $11v - 1 = 1 - 11v$

(D) $7v + 77 = 77 + 7v$

11. Which of the below graphs represents the equation of the straight line represented as

$$y = \frac{4}{5}x + 3$$

(A)

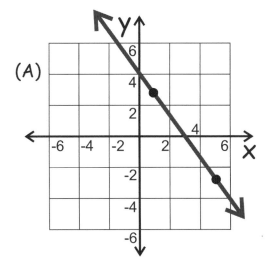

(B)

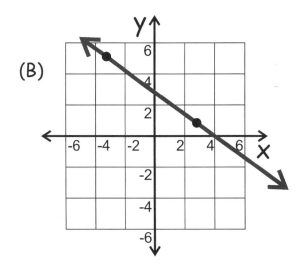

(C)

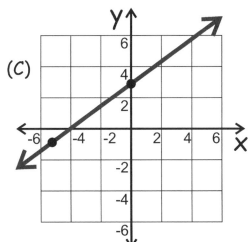

(D)

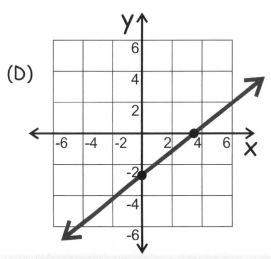

www.a4ace.com   www.math-knots.com

12. SHAKTI team raises funds for underprivileged girls education by organizing a cultural show. They sell each ticket for $11 and the rent of the space is $1500 . If P is the profit and T is the price of the ticket as shown by the given equation

$$P = 11 \, T - 1500$$

What is the y-intercept of the equation ?

(A)   -1500   (B) 150

(C)   1500   (D)   11

13. Roots of the below equation are
$$p^2 - 3p - 64 = 0$$

(A)   (-9 , -6)
(B)   (9 , 6)
(C)   (-9 , 6)
(D)   (9 , -6)

14. Find the equation of the straight line with slope = $\frac{1}{3}$ and containing the point (0 , -3)

(A) $y = \frac{x}{3} - 3$ (B) $y = \frac{x}{3} + 3$

(C) $y = x - 9$ (D) $y = x - 3$

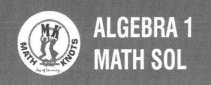

15. Which of the below inequalities is same as 8m + 3n =< 15

   (A) $n < \dfrac{8m}{3} - 5$

   (B) $n > 5 - \dfrac{8m}{3}$

   (C) $n =< 5 - \dfrac{8m}{3}$

   (D) $n < 5 - 8m$

16. What is the slope of the line that passes through

$$(20 , -6) , (3 , 1)$$

   (A) $\dfrac{17}{17}$

   (B) $\dfrac{-17}{7}$

   (C) $\dfrac{17}{7}$

   (D) $\dfrac{-7}{17}$

17. Rosy has 90 pieces of candies to distribute among her friends. She gave four to each of her friend. She only have 10 remaining.
   How many friends does she have ?

   (A) 35
   (B) 20
   (C) 24
   (D) 30

 www.a4ace.com   www.math-knots.com

18. Ten Rose plants and 1 ever green tree costs $100.90. 3 Rose plants and one ever green tree cost $34.40. Cost of one Rose plant is ?

(A) $9.30
(B) $5.30
(C) $7.20
(D) $9.50

19. Evaluate -5 ((-10 / 2) + p + q) ; Where p = -4 and q = -7

(A) 75
(B) 7
(C) 3.50
(D) 80

20. Evaluate

$$(7.11 \times 10^{5}) (3 \times 10^{-2})$$

(A) 0.0213×10^{2}

(B) 21.33×10^{3}

(C) 0.213×10^{15}

(D) 0.2233×10^{-3}

28   www.a4ace.com   www.math-knots.com

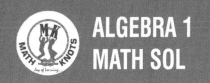

21. Simplify the expression
$$(1 + 7v^5 - 13v^3) + (-4 - 9v^3 - 12v^5)$$

(A) $-12v^5 - 12v^3 - 3$

(B) $-12v^5 - 22v^3 - 3$

(C) $-12v^2 - 16v^3 - 3$

(D) $-5v^5 - 22v^3 - 3$

22. Simplest radical form of $\sqrt{405}$ is ?

(A) $9\sqrt{3}$

(B) $8\sqrt{5}$

(C) $9\sqrt{5}$

(D) $\sqrt{8}$

23. Evaluate the polynomial to simplest form where $n \neq 0$
$$(45n^6 + 36n^5 + 9n^4) \div 9n^2$$

(A) $5n^4 + 4n^3 + n^2$

(B) $4\dfrac{n^2}{9} - \dfrac{5n}{9} - \dfrac{1}{9}$

(C) $\dfrac{n^2}{7} + \dfrac{4n}{3} + 2$

(D) $\dfrac{n^2}{3} + \dfrac{n}{4} + 4$

24. Factorize the below quadratic expression completely ?
$$7v^2 + 22v + 16$$

(A) $(v - 8)(7v + 2)$

(B) $(7v + 8)(v + 2)$

(C) $(7v - 10)(v + 6)$

(D) $(7v + 8)(5v + 2)$

   www.a4ace.com   www.math-knots.com

25. The product of t and 6 is less than or equal to 42

   (A) 6t <= 42   (B) t - 6 <= 42

   (B) t - 6 < = 42   (D) t^2 <= 42

26. Evaluate the polynomial
$$5x^2(x^2 - 3x + 6)$$

   (A) $24x^3 + 24x^2 + 21x$ (B) $6x^2 - 24x - 12$

   (C) $5x^4 - 15x^3 + 30x^2$ (D) $24x^2 - 42x - 36$

27. Which labeled point on the number line is closest to $\sqrt{118}$

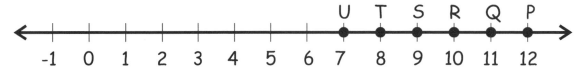

   (A) U   (B) S   (C) Q   (D) T

28. A cell phone cover has two flaps side. One flap is of the length
8.92×10^{-6} and the other is 1.60×10^{-6}
What is the difference in the lengths of flaps ?

   (A) 7.32×10^{-6} (B) 0.732×10^{-6}

   (C) 0.0732×10^{-6} (D) 73.2×10^{-6}

30   www.a4ace.com   www.math-knots.com

29. Factorize the below quadratic expression completely ?

$$-12k^2 - 14k$$

(A) $-2(3 - k^2)$

(B) $-3(6 + 7k^2)$

(C) $-2(6 - 7k)$

(D) $-2k(6k + 7)$

30. The product of p and 9 is less than 29

(A) $\dfrac{9}{p} < 29$

(B) $p \cdot 9 < 29$

(C) $\dfrac{p}{9} < 29$

(D) $p^9 < 29$

31. The function f(y) = 35 + 15 h represents the amount of money, in dollars. where h is the no of hours Shan worked. He works 10 hours this week. How much money did he earn this week ?

(A)   165

(B)   225

(C)   185

(D)   180

32. Which of the below equation represents the relationship between time and number of hoops made ?

Time in minutes (t)	Hoops (h)
5	10
10	20
15	30
20	40
25	50

(A) h = 2 t

(B) h = 2 + t

(C) h = $\dfrac{t}{2}$

(D) t - 2

33. Find the domain of the relation shown from the below data set ?

X	Y
-3	-9
-1	-3
2	6
7	21
11	33

(A) { -3 , -1 , 2 , 7 , 11 }

(B) { -3 , 11 , 0 , 7 , 5 }

(C) { -9 , -3 , 2 , 7 , 21 }

(D) { -1 , -3 , 6 , -7 , 21 }

34. A journey of 120 miles costs $36. How much will a journey of 200 miles cost ?

    (A) $ 56   (B) $ 60

    (C) $ 45   (D) $ 65

35. Which of the below order pairs data set represents a function ?

    (A) { (3.8 , 3) , (5.9 , 9) , (12.7, 32) , (15.6 , 54) , (5.9 , 31) }

    (B) { (3.8 , 3) , (5.9 , 9) , (12.7 , 32) , (3.8 , 54) , (17, 31) }

    (C) { (3.8 , 3) , (5.9 , 9) , (12.7 , 32) , (15.6 , 54) , (17, 31) }

    (D) { (-15.6 , 3) , (5.9 , 9) , (12.7, 32) , (-15.6 , 54) , (17, 31) }

36. Evaluate f(5) , where $f(x) = 2x^3 - 5x$

    (A) 225

    (B) 200

    (C) 250

    (D) 100

37. What is the domain of the function y = x + 2 represented by the below graph ?

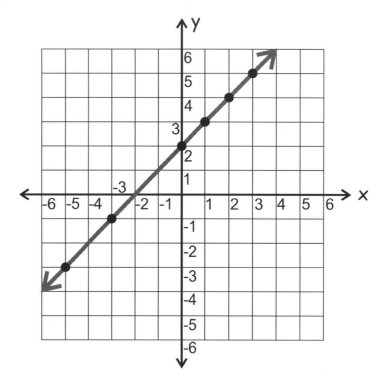

(A)   D = { 0 , 1 , 2 , 3 , - 5 , -3 }

(B)   D = { 3.5 , 4 , 1.7 , -2 , 5.2 }

(C)   D = { 0.7 , 1 , -2.5 , 5 , -6.9 }

(D)   D = { 7 , 2.5 , 3.5 , - 6 , -5 }

38. What is the range of the function f(x) = -2x^2 + 7
    where Domain = { -3 , 0 , 1 , 5}

(A) { -11 , 7 , 5 , -43}

(B) { -11 , 7 , 5 , 43}

(C) { 11 , 7 , 5 , 43}

(D) { -11 , 17 , 25 , -43}

39. Which graph best represents a direct variation ?

$$y = 2x$$

(A)

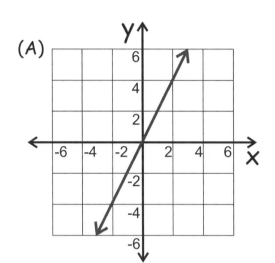

(B)

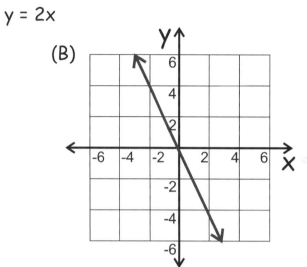

(C)

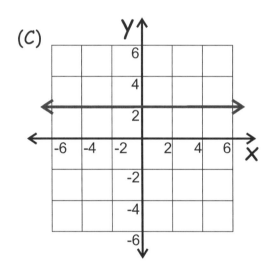

(D)

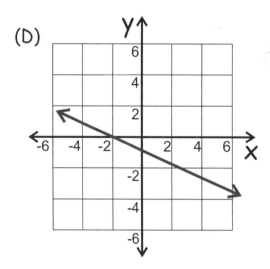

40. Which of the below tables shows the relation between X and Y as direct variation.

(A)

X	Y
1	1
3	2
5	12
7	3
9	9

(B)

X	Y
1	1
3	3
5	11
7	7
9	9

(C)

X	Y
1	3
3	9
5	15
7	21
9	27

(D)

X	Y
1	11
3	20
5	12
7	30
9	90

41. Cost of each art piece in the art exhibition is shown in the below table.

# of Art pieces (P)	sale prices $(S)
1	15
4	60
8	120
10	150
12	180

Which of the below gives the total price (T) of "P" art pieces ?

(A) T = 15 P

(B) T = 15 - P

(C) T = 15 + P

(D) T = 10 P

42. Which of the below graph best represents the function
$$f(x) = x^2 + 5x + 4$$

(A)
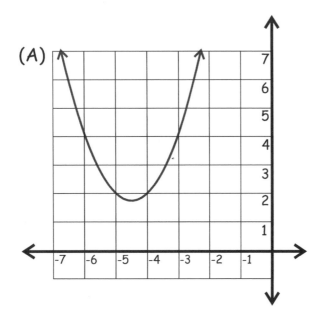

(B)
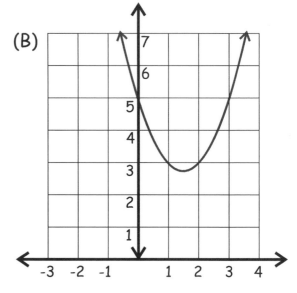

(C)
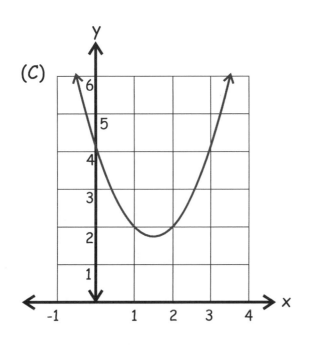

(D)
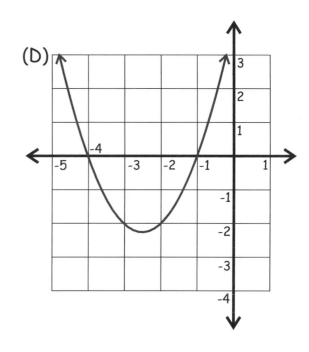

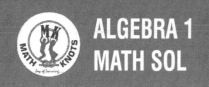
43. Find the sum of the below matrices ?

$$\begin{vmatrix} 5 & 7 \\ -2 & -4 \\ 1 & 6 \end{vmatrix} \quad + \quad \begin{vmatrix} 11 & 9 \\ 15 & 8 \\ 3 & -1 \end{vmatrix}$$

(A) $\begin{vmatrix} 15 & -5 \\ 10 & 20 \\ -3 & -1 \end{vmatrix}$

(B) $\begin{vmatrix} 16 & 16 \\ 13 & 4 \\ 4 & 5 \end{vmatrix}$

(C) $\begin{vmatrix} 7 & 17 \\ -8 & 9 \\ 5 & -4 \end{vmatrix}$

(D) $\begin{vmatrix} 10 & -12 \\ 16 & -6 \\ 2 & -11 \end{vmatrix}$

44. The table below shows the temperatures in various cities in USA during December.

December temperatures (Degrees Celsius)

Day	Virginia	Newyork	Pittsburg	Chicago
Monday	-1	-5	-3	0
Tuesday	0	-7	7	-1
Wednesday	-3	-6	11	-7
Thursday	-2	-9	-9	-2
Friday	5	-2	-1	5
Saturday	7	5	-3	4
Sunday	0	-3	-2	-2

Which state had the highest mean temperature this week ?

(A) Chicago

(B) Pittsburg

(C) Virginia

(D) New York

45. Which equation is the line of best fit for the data in the below table ?

X	Y
1	2
3	3
6	5
7	6
8	6

(A) $Y = \dfrac{2x}{3} + 1$

(B) $Y = \dfrac{2x}{3} - 1$

(C) $Y = \dfrac{4x}{3} - 1$

(D) $Y = \dfrac{5x}{3} + 2$

46. Which graph best represents the below data

Student Name	Puzzles Solved	Student Name	Puzzles Solved
William	44	Laurel	61
James	53	Olivia	54
Tom	56	Ava	55
Logan	54	Sophia	50
Mark	46	Mia	46
Benjamin	45	Emma	59
John	50	Lucas	41
Donald	34	Henry	54
Barak	64	Carter	40
George	50	Luke	60
Harry	65	Anthony	43
Oliver	50		

(A)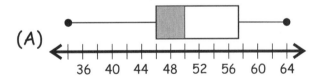

(B)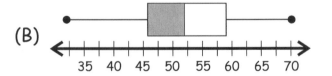

(C)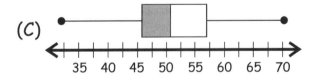

(D)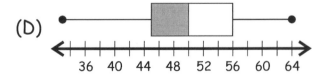

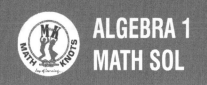
47.   Which graph best represents a direct variation

$$y = \frac{7}{4}x - 3$$

(A)
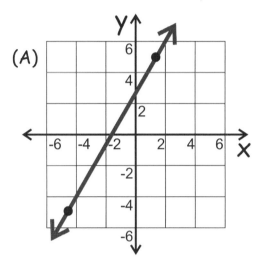

(B)
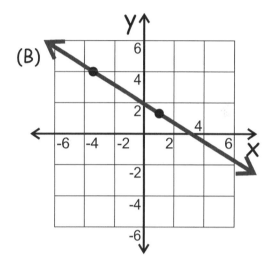

(C)
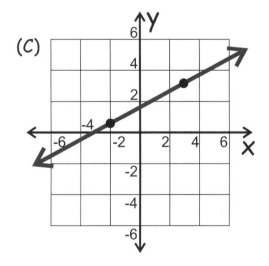

(D)
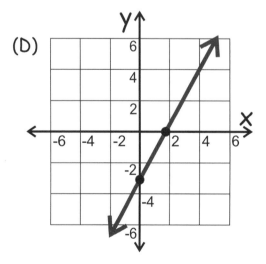

48. Dora solved puzzles each day over spring break. The number of puzzles she solved in six days is shown.

13 , 11 , 13 , 15 , 10 , 13 , 9

She then solved 15 more puzzles on last day. How are the mean and median affected ?

(A) The mean increased and the median remained the same.
(B) The median increased and the mean remained the same.
(C) The median and the mean both remained the same.
(D) The mean and the median both decreased.

49. ABC online game store charges $7 shipping per game ordered
The table below shows various games and their prices.

Types	X - Box Game	Y - Box Game
Sports #1	55	32
Adventure #2	48	41
Exercise #3	63	59

Jack orders two games each Which of the below represents the total bill ?

(A) $10 \begin{vmatrix} 25 & 30 \\ 45 & 39 \\ 42 & 68 \end{vmatrix}$

(B) $14 \begin{vmatrix} 55 & 32 \\ 48 & 41 \\ 63 & 59 \end{vmatrix}$

(C) $7 \begin{vmatrix} 55 & 32 \\ 48 & 41 \\ 63 & 59 \end{vmatrix}$

(D) $20 \begin{vmatrix} 38 & 41 \\ 56 & 21 \\ 56 & 77 \end{vmatrix}$

50. Evaluate the below matrices

$$\begin{vmatrix} -6 & 1 \\ 4 & 3 \\ 0 & 5 \end{vmatrix} - \begin{vmatrix} 9 & 3 \\ -2 & 0 \\ 3 & 1 \end{vmatrix} = ?$$

(A) $\begin{vmatrix} 15 & 8 \\ 5 & 4 \\ 9 & 7 \end{vmatrix}$

(B) $\begin{vmatrix} -15 & -2 \\ 6 & 3 \\ -3 & 4 \end{vmatrix}$

(C) $\begin{vmatrix} 14 & 7 \\ 2 & -13 \\ 15 & -21 \end{vmatrix}$

(D) $\begin{vmatrix} -9 & 15 \\ 7 & 17 \\ 15 & -1 \end{vmatrix}$

www.a4ace.com   www.math-knots.com

ALGEBRA 1
SOL
Practice Test - 2

1.   Solve for v

$$2 (v - 1) = -1 (-3 - v)$$

(A) 2   (B) -6   (C) 6   (D) 5

2.   If f(k) = 5k - 9 then which of the below best describes the graph f(k)

(A) Slope = 5 ,   y-intercept = 9
(B) Slope = - 3 ,   y-intercept = 1
(C) Slope = - 5 ,   y-intercept = -9
(D) Slope = 5 ,   y-intercept = -9

3.   Find the slope of the line in the graph below

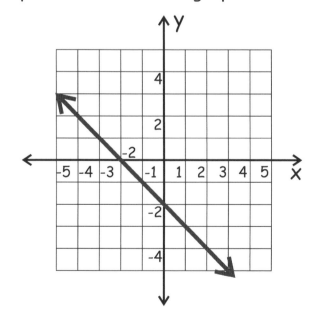

(A) 1   (B) -2   (C) -1   (D) 2

4. Which of the below order pair is the solution of the below system of equations?

$$5p + q = 1$$
$$2p - q = -8$$

(A) (1 , 6)   (B) (-1 , -7)   (C) (-6 , 7)   (D) (-1 , 6)

5. -4 (-6 + 4m) <= 152

(A) m >= -23   (B) m >= -8   (C) m >= 10   (D) m <= -8

6. The equation of the line 'm' is represented by which of the below options ?

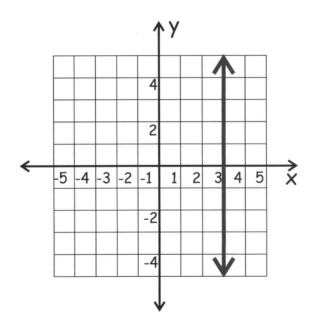

(A) y = -3x   (B) x = 3

(C) y = 3x   (D) x = -3

              www.a4ace.com   www.math-knots.com

7. Which of the below quadratic equation has roots of 1 and 12 ?

(A) $h^2 - 13h + 12 = 0$　　　　　(B) $h^2 + 13h + 12 = 0$

(C) $h^2 + 12h + 13 = 0$　　　　　(D) $h^2 + 4h - 12 = 0$

8. Which Graph best represents the equation

$$y = \frac{5}{3}x$$

(A)
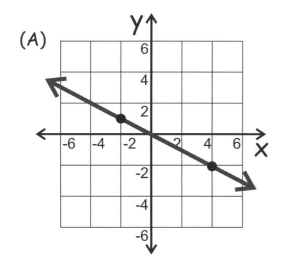

(B)
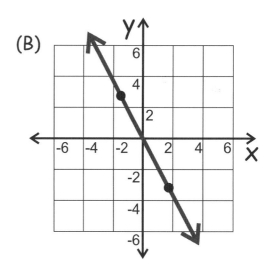

(C)
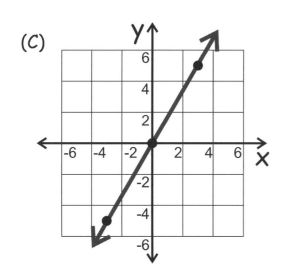

(D)
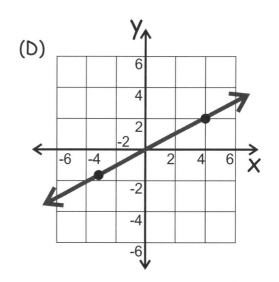

9. System of linear equations are shown in the graph below. Which of the below is the solution of the system of linear equations ?

$$y = \frac{1}{7} x - 8$$

$$y = \frac{6}{7} x - 3$$

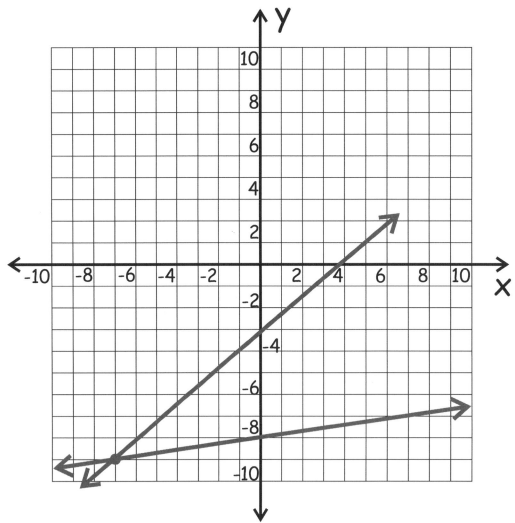

(A) (-7 , 9)

(B) (-6 , -9)

(C) (-9 , -6)

(D) (-7 , -9)

10. Which of the below represents distributive property ?

   (A) 6 (8 + 8k) = 8 (6 - 6 k)   (B) 48 + 48k = 48 (1 - k)

   (C) 4 + 48k = 48k - 8   (D) 6 (8 + 8k) = 48 + 48k

11. Which of the below graphs represents the equation of the straight line
   represented as

$$y = -2x + 1$$

(A)
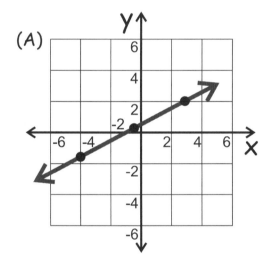

(B)
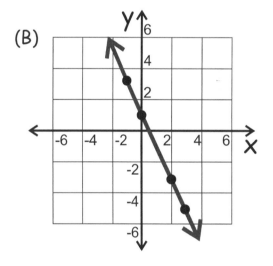

(C)
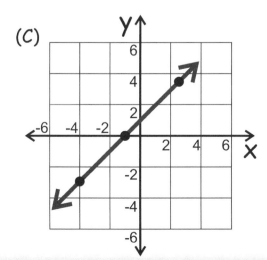

(D)
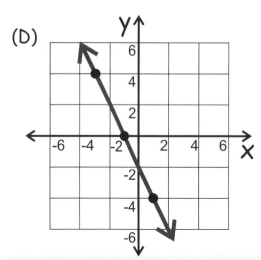

12. Tony buys a house for $535,000 and no deposits are made into his savings account, after a week the balance of his account can be obtained by the below equation

$$B = 125W - 535{,}000$$

What is the slope of the equation ?

(A) -535,000   (B) -125

(C) 125   (D) 535,000

13. Roots of the below equation are

$$v^2 - 9v + 20$$

(A) (4 , 5)

(B) (6 , 7)

(C) (3 , 5)

(D) (2 , 6)

14. Find the equation of the straight line with slope = $\dfrac{4}{5}$ and containing the point (5 , 6)

(A) $y = \dfrac{4x}{5} - 2$ (B) $y = \dfrac{x}{5} - 6$

(C) $y = \dfrac{x}{3} + 6$ (D) $y = \dfrac{4x}{5} + 2$

15. Which of the below inequalities is same as 3m - 4n < (20)

(A) $n < 5 - \dfrac{3m}{4}$ (B) $n > 5 - \dfrac{3m}{2}$

(C) $n > \dfrac{3m}{4} - 5$ (D) $n < 5 + 3m$

16. What is the slope of the line that passes through

(6 , -9) and (6 , 2)

(A) $\dfrac{2}{3}$ (B) Undefined

(C) 0   (D) $\dfrac{-2}{3}$

17. Tanya won 45 super puzzles at school carnival. She gave three to each of her cousins and has 6 remaining. How many cousins does she have in all ?

(A) 24

(B) 16

(C) 9

(D) 13

18. The sum of two numbers is 12.1. Their difference is 1.7
Which is the smallest number ?

(A) 5.2
(B) 3.6
(C) 9.3
(D) 4.5

19. Evaluate $y + x + (y^2)^2$; Where x = 1 , y = -2

(A) 14
(B) 26
(C) 5
(D) 15

20. Evaluate

$$(0.7 \times 10^8)(8.5 \times 10^6)$$

(A) 0.8235×10^0

(B) 8.235×10^{14}

(C) 5.95×10^{14}

(D) 0.595×10^0

21. Simplify the expression

$$(2 + 9x^3 - 13x^5) + (-2x^5 - 11x^3 - 9)$$

(A) $-15x^5 - 2x^3 - 7$ (B) $-15x^5 - 2x^3 - 11$

(C) $-15x^5 + x^3 - 11$ (D) $-20x^5 + x^3 - 11$

22. Simplest radical form of $\sqrt{768}$ is ?

(A) 16   (B) $16\sqrt{2}$

(C) $8\sqrt{3}$ (D) $16\sqrt{3}$

23. Evaluate the polynomial to simplest form where $x \neq 0$
$$(n^3 + 12n^2 + 3n) \div 6n$$

(A) $\dfrac{n}{3} + 4 + \dfrac{1}{n}$ (B) $\dfrac{n}{4} + 15 + \dfrac{3}{n}$

(C) $\dfrac{n^2}{2} + 2n + 18$ (D) $\dfrac{n^2}{6} + 2n + \dfrac{1}{2}$

24. Factorize the below quadratic expression completely ?
$$10n^2 + 4n + 28$$

(A) $(10n^2 + 4n + 28) / 2$ (B) $2(5n + 2)(n-7)$

(C) $2(5n^2 + 2n + 14)$ (D) $(3n - 10)(n + 5)$

25. 8 less than c is 22

   (A) $c - 8 = 22$ (B) $8c = 22$

   (C) $c^2 + 8 = 22$ (D) $8 - c = 22$

26. Evaluate the polynomial

$$7m (5m^2 + 8m + 3)$$

   (A) $40m^3 + 140m^2 - 15$ (B) $12m^4 + 18m^3 - 16m^2 + 9$

   (C) $35m^4 - 56m^3 - 21m^2$ (D) $35m^3 + 56m^2 + 21m$

27. Which labeled point on the number line is closest to $\sqrt{97}$

   (A)   P   (B)   R   (C)   T   (D)   Q

28. A hand bag has two handles. One handle is of the length 45.34×10^{-3} inches and the shorter one is 31.29×10^{-3}. What is the difference in the lengths of the flaps ?

   (A) 15.05×10^{-3} (B) 14.005×10^{-3}

   (C) 14.05×10^{-3} (D) 14.04×10^{-3}

                   www.a4ace.com   www.math-knots.com

29. Factorize the below quadratic expression completely?

$$70n^6 + 40n^2$$

(A) $10n^2 (35n^5 - 10n)$

(B) $10n^2 (14n^2 - 8n)$

(C) $40n^2 (7n^4 - 4)$

(D) $10n^2 (7n^4 + 4)$

30. The product of r and 5 is greater than or equal to 5

(A) $r^2 + 5 \geq 5$

(B) $5r \geq 5$

(C) $r^5 \geq 5$

(D) $r - 5 \geq 5$

31. The function f(y) = (5/3) m, represents the amount of muffins baked by Beth. Where m is the no of muffins she gave to her friends.
If she shares 24 muffins with her friends, How many muffins did she make originally ?

(A) 44

(B) 38

(C) 25

(D) 40

32. Which of the below equation represents the relationship between time and Cookies made with an additional preparation time of 45 minutes ?

Time in minutes (t)	# cookies (c)
3	12
4	16
8	32
10	40
24	96

(A) c = 4 t   (B) c = 45 - 4 t   (C) c = 4t/45   (D) c = 4t + 45

33. Find the domain of the relation shown from the below data set?

x	y
-27	-2
-19	-8
4	9
16	11
19	14

(A) { -2 , -8 , 11 , 9, 14 }

(B) { -2 , -8 , 9 , -7 , 21 }

(C) { -27, -19 , 4 , 16 , 19 }

(D) { -11, -27 , 4 , 16 , 14 }

34   If the thickness of a pile of 80 cardboards is 117.20 mm (milli meters) ,
      how many card boards will there be in a pile which is 703.20 mm thick ?

   (A) 488   (B) 480

   (C) 670   (D) 467

35.   Which of the below order pairs data set represents a function ?

   (A)   { (10 , 7) , (5.8 , 11) , (7.8 , 22) , (10 , 27) , (15.7 , 41) }

   (B)   { (4.3 , 7) , (5.8 , 11) , (5.8 , 22) , (10 , 27) , (15.7 , 41) }

   (C)   { (4.3 , 7) , (5.8 , 11) , (7.8 , 22) , (10 , 27) , (15.7 , 41) }

   (D)   { (-4.3 , 7) , (5.8 , 11) , (7.8 , 22) , (10 , 27) , (-4.3 , 41) }

36.   Evaluate f(4), where $f(x) = \dfrac{3x^4}{16} - 5x$

   (A)   91

   (B)   20

   (C)   13

   (D)   28

37. What is the domain of the function y = x + 1 represented by the below graph ?

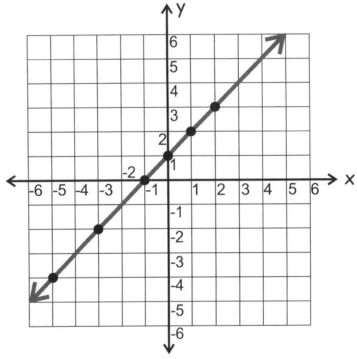

(A) D = {0 , 1 , -1 , 2 , - 5 , -3 }

(B) D = {7.7 , -1 , 4.5 , 15.8 , 8 }

(C) D = {0.9 , 1 , -2 , 5.7 , -3 }

(D) D = {9 , -1 , 2 , - 7.5 , -3 }

38. What is the range of the function f(x) = x^2 - 8x + 4
where Domain = { -7 , -2 , 3 , 4}

(A) { -109 , -24 , -11 , -12}

(B) { 1009 , 24 , -11 , -102}

(C) { 109 , 24 , -11 , -12}

(D) { 109 , -24 , -10 , -14}

39. Which graph best represents a direct variation ?

$$y = x$$

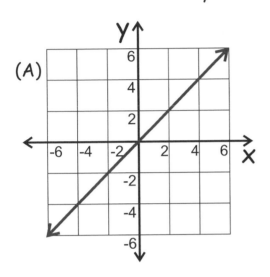

(A)

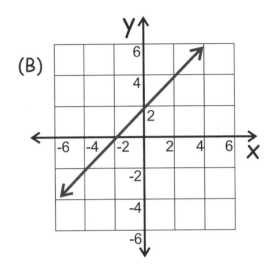

(B)

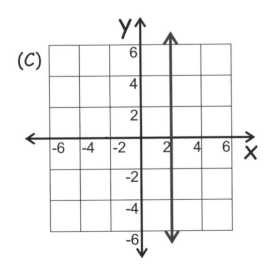

(C)

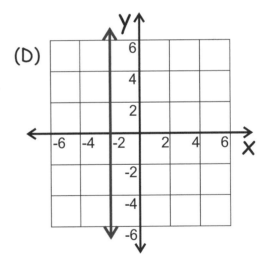

(D)

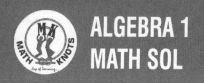

40. Which of the below tables shows the relation between X and Y as direct variation ?

(A)

x	y
2	5
4	10
6	15
8	20
10	25

(B)

x	y
2	1
4	13
6	11
8	13
10	9

(C)

x	y
2	2
4	11
6	20
8	14
10	18

(D)

x	y
2	100
4	204
6	102
8	300
10	140

41. Cost of each STEM kit in the STEAM expo is shown in the below table with a flat rate of $3 sales tax on each kit sold.

# of STEM kitc (S)	sale prices $(P)
1	34
4	136
8	272
10	340
12	408

Which of the below gives the total price (t) of "S" STEM kits ?

(A)   T = 37 P - 3S

(B)   T = 34 P- 3S

(C)   T = 37 S

(D)   T = 134P + 3S

42. Which of the below graph best represents the function

$$f(x) = x^2 + 9x + 18$$

(A)
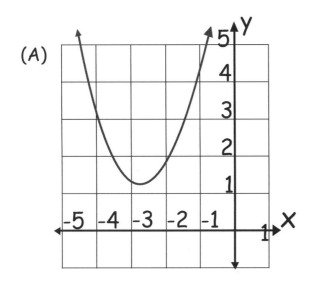

(B)
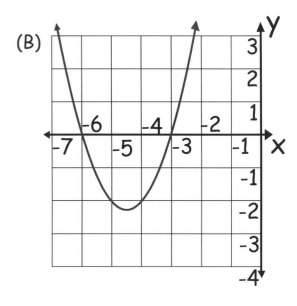

(C)
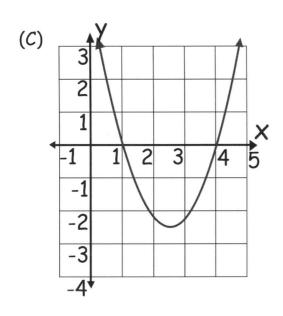

(D)
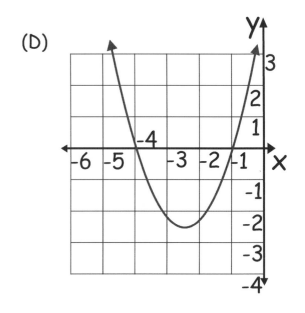

43. Find the sum of the below Matrices ?

$$\begin{vmatrix} 1 & 8 \\ -3 & -5 \\ 7 & 12 \end{vmatrix} - \begin{vmatrix} -10 & 2 \\ -1 & 0 \\ 6 & -17 \end{vmatrix}$$

(A) $\begin{vmatrix} 11 & 6 \\ -2 & -5 \\ 1 & 29 \end{vmatrix}$ (B) $\begin{vmatrix} -7 & 10 \\ -4 & -5 \\ 13 & 5 \end{vmatrix}$

(C) $\begin{vmatrix} 15 & 1 \\ 7 & 8 \\ 5 & 16 \end{vmatrix}$ (D) $\begin{vmatrix} 15 & 4 \\ -6 & 6 \\ 3 & -2 \end{vmatrix}$

44. The table below shows the XYZ car sales in various stores in Virginia

February car sales

Day	Store#1	Store#2	Store#3	Store#4
Monday	51	11	17	31
Tuesday	82	32	4	14
Wednesday	17	15	1	0
Thursday	22	0	31	7
Friday	33	9	69	6
Saturday	15	52	15	15
Sunday	30	33	25	9

Which store had the greatest mean sales during this week ?

(A) Store # 2
(B) Store # 3
(C) Store # 1
(D) Store # 4

45. Which equation is the line of best fit for the data in the below table ?

x	y
1	5.5
2	6
6	8
8	9
9	10.5

(A) $y = \dfrac{x}{3} + 5$ (B) $y = \dfrac{2x}{3} - 1$

(C) $y = \dfrac{4x}{3} - 1$ (D) $y = \dfrac{x}{2} + 5$

         www.a4ace.com   www.math-knots.com

46. Which graph best represents the below data ?

Soccer Tournament 2019

Team Name	Goals made
Predators	8
Rebels	4
Red devils	12
Profs	17
Aces	1
All Blacks	3
Red dragons	17
Red foxes	6
Friars	1
Fusion	5
Bandits	6
Lady hawks	8
Lady birds	1
United	2
Lady Eagles	9

Team Name	Goals made
Battlers	4
Big blues	16
Black stars	1
Antelopes	2
Colonels	10
Comets	4
Captains	5

(A)
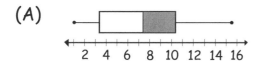

(B)
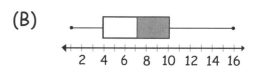

(C)
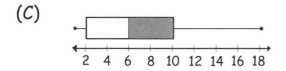

(D)
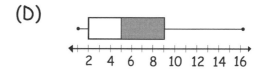

69   www.a4ace.com   www.math-knots.com

47. Which is most likely the best fit for the below equation ?

$$y = -\frac{4}{5}x - 1$$

(A)
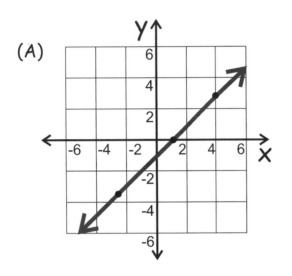

(B)
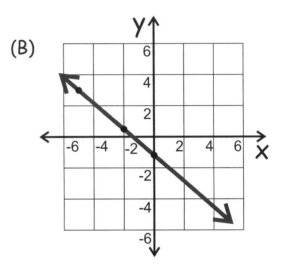

(C)
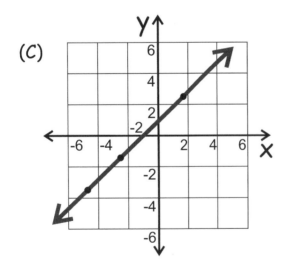

(D)
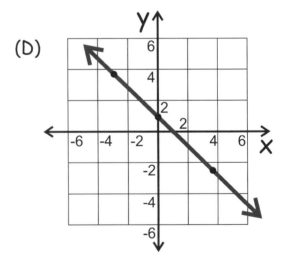

70   www.a4ace.com   www.math-knots.com

48. Tim's car sales each week over last 5 weeks in summer are shown
$$54 , 31 , 53 , 65 , 17$$
He then sold 29 more cars. How are the mean and median affected ?

(A) The mean increased and the median remained the same.
(B) The median decreased and the mean is decreased.
(C) The median and the mean both remained the same.
(D) The mean and the median both increased.

49. ABC sports store charges $9 shipping per sports equipment ordered
The table below shows various sports equipment and their prices.

Item Name	Cost ($)	Item Name	Cost ($)
Basket Ball	11	Tennis Racquet	99
Soccer	12	Bicycle	121
Foot ball	9	Tread Mill	321

(A)
$$9 \begin{vmatrix} 11 & 99 \\ 12 & 121 \\ 9 & 321 \end{vmatrix}$$

(B)
$$7 \begin{vmatrix} 11 & 99 \\ 12 & 121 \\ 9 & 321 \end{vmatrix}$$

(C)
$$10 \begin{vmatrix} 25 & 30 \\ 45 & 39 \\ 42 & 68 \end{vmatrix}$$

(D)
$$20 \begin{vmatrix} 38 & 41 \\ 56 & 21 \\ 56 & 77 \end{vmatrix}$$

50. Evaluate the below

$$
\begin{vmatrix} 9 & 0 \\ 4 & 5 \\ 7 & -3 \end{vmatrix} - \begin{vmatrix} 5 & 3 \\ 2 & 1 \\ 3 & 7 \end{vmatrix} = ?
$$

(A) $\begin{vmatrix} 4 & -3 \\ 2 & 4 \\ 4 & -10 \end{vmatrix}$

(B) $\begin{vmatrix} 10 & 6 \\ 5 & 4 \\ 7 & 0 \end{vmatrix}$

(C) $\begin{vmatrix} 10 & -6 \\ 2 & -3 \\ 15 & -21 \end{vmatrix}$

(D) $\begin{vmatrix} -9 & 5 \\ 7 & 17 \\ 18 & -1 \end{vmatrix}$

ALGEBRA 1
SOL
Practice Test - 3

1.   Solve for v

$$-1(v + 2) = -2(1 - 5v)$$

(A) 0   (B) 7   (C) -9   (D) 5

2.   If f(k) = -11k - 33 then which of the below best describes the graph f(k)

(A) Slope = 9   , y-intercept = -33
(B) Slope = -11 , y-intercept = 33
(C) Slope = -33 , y-intercept = -11
(D) Slope = -11 , y-intercept = -33

3.   Find the slope of the line in the graph below

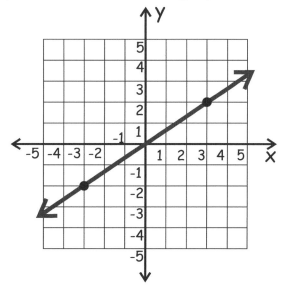

(A) $-\dfrac{2}{3}$ (B) $\dfrac{5}{3}$

(C) $\dfrac{2}{3}$ (D) $\dfrac{2}{3}$

4. Which of the below order pair is the solution of the below system of equations ?

$$3p - 2q = -2$$
$$p + 2q = 18$$

(A) (11 , 7)   (B) (4 , 7)   (C) (-4 , -7)   (D) (0 , 7)

5. $106 <= (5 (4m + 5)) + 7m$

(A) m <= 2
(B) m <= -12
(C) m >= 12
(D) m >= 3

6. The equation of the line 'm' is represented by which of the below options ?

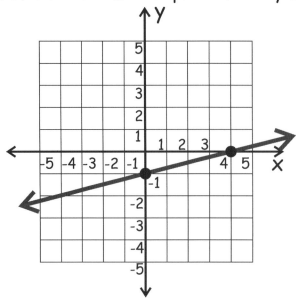

(A) $y = -\frac{1}{4}x + 1$

(B) $y = -\frac{1}{2}x - 1$

(C) $y = \frac{1}{4}x - 1$

(D) $y = -x + \frac{1}{4}$

7. Which of the below quadratic equation has roots of 7 and 11 ?

    (A) $g^2 - 18g + 77 = 0$ (B) $g^2 + 18g + 77 = 0$

    (C) $g^2 + 18g - 77 = 0$ (D) $g^2 - 18g - 77 = 0$

8. Which Graph best represents the equation

    $$Y = -3x - 2$$

(A)

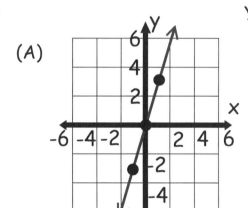

(B)

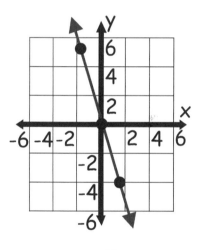

(C)

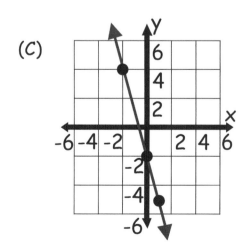

(D)

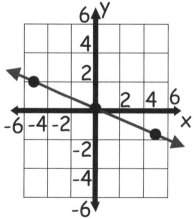

9. System of linear equations are shown in the graph below. Which of the below is the solution of the system of linear equations?

$$y = \frac{4}{7}x + 8$$

$$y = -\frac{9}{7}x - 5$$

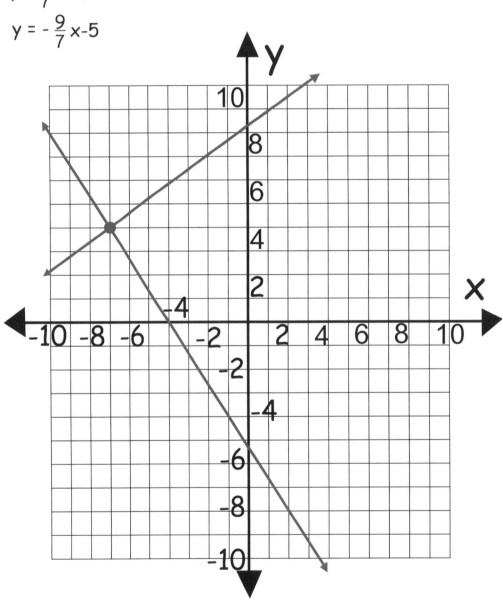

(A) (4 , 4)   (B) (-7 , 4)   (C) (-4 , 4)   (D) (-4 , -4)

         www.a4ace.com   www.math-knots.com

10. Which of the below represents distributive property

   (A)   -4(5m - 3) = -20m + 12   (B)   -4(5m - 3) = -20m - 12

   (C)   -4(5m - 3) = 20m + 12   (D)   -4(5m - 3) = 2(-10m - 6)

11. Which of the below graphs represents the equation of the straight line
    represented as
    $$y = -\frac{4}{3}x - 5$$

(A)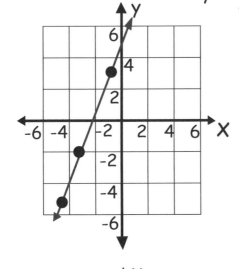

(B)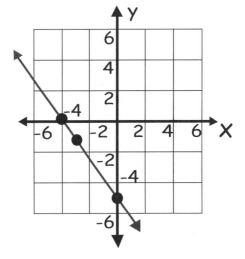

(C)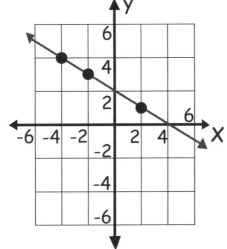

(D)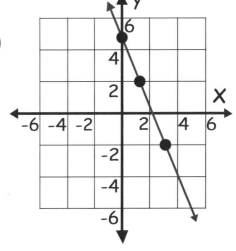

                   www.a4ace.com   www.math-knots.com

12. Super STEAM team rises funds for the school STEAM laboratory. They sell home baked cupcakes for $3 each. The cost of the ingredients is $205. If P is the profit and M is the number of cupcakes sold as given by the below equation

$$P = 3M - 205$$

What is the slope of the equation ?

(A) 3   (B) -205

(C) 205   (D) -3

13. Roots of the below equation are

$$p^2 + 6p + 9 = 0$$

(A) (3 , -3)   (B) (3 , 3)

(C) (-3 , 3)   (D) (-3 , -3)

14. Find the equation of the straight line with slope = 3 and containing the point (8 , 2)

(A) s = 3p + 22   (B) s = 3p - 22

(C) s = 22p + 3   (D) $s = \dfrac{p}{3} + 22$

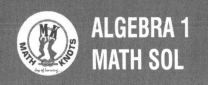

15. Which of the below inequalities is same as 5m - 2n >= (-10)

(A) $n <= 5 + \dfrac{5m}{3}$

(B) $n >= 5 - \dfrac{5}{2} m$

(C) $n <= 5m + \dfrac{5}{2}$

(D) $n <= 5 + \dfrac{5}{2} m$

16. What is the slope of the line that passes through (-20 , -11) and (15 , -4)

(A) $\dfrac{1}{5}$

(B) $-\dfrac{1}{5}$

(C) 5

(D) -5

17. Tina bought a Book for $7 and seven pens. She spent a total of $42. Cost of each pen is ?

(A) $5

(B) $7

(C) $1

(D) $4

18. John bought 2 adult tickets and one child ticket at Fairfax carnival for $30.50. Lucy bought 3 adult tickets and one child ticket at Fairfax carnival for $40.40. What is the price of the adult ticket ?

    (A) $10.45   (B) $8.90

    (C) $9.90   (D) $6.10

19. Evaluate $h + \dfrac{j\,(h-h)}{27}$; Where h = -11 , and j = -3

    (A)   -11

    (B)   -3

    (C)   -8

    (D)   11

20. Evaluate the below

    $$(4.2 \times 10^{3})\ (6.45 \times 10^{-6})$$

    (A) 2.709×10^{-3}

    (B) 12.709×10^{2}

    (C) 12.709×10^{3}

    (D) 2.709×10^{-2}

21. Simplify the expression

$$(x^2 - x - 5) + (2x + 4 - 4x^4) + (7x^2 - 4x^4 + 3x)$$

(A) $-6x^4 - 8x^2 - 4x - 1$ (B) $-6x^4 - 3x^2 - 8x - 1$

(C) $-8x^4 + 8x^2 + 4x - 1$ (D) $-6x^4 + 8x^2 + 4x + 1$

22. Simplest radical form of $\sqrt{867}$ is ?

(A) $17\sqrt{3}$ (B) 17

(C) $17\sqrt{7}$ (D) $17\sqrt{2}$

23. Evaluate the polynomial to simplest form where $x \neq 0$

$$(12x^5 + 12x^4 + 6x^3) \div 6x^3$$

(A) $2 + \dfrac{1}{x} + \dfrac{1}{x^2}$ (B) $2x^2 + 2x + 1$

(C) $\dfrac{x^2}{4} + \dfrac{x}{2} + \dfrac{3}{4}$ (D) $4x^2 - x + 1$

24. Factorize the below quadratic expression completely ?

$$6r^2 - 22r + 16$$

(A) $2(5r - 4)(r - 7)$ (B) $2(3r - 8)(r - 1)$

(C) $4(3r + 10)(r + 10)$ (D) $r(3r + 2)$

 www.a4ace.com   www.math-knots.com

25. Half of a number is greater than or equal to 35

    (A) $n - 2 \geq 35$ (B) $n + 2 \geq 35$

    (C) $\frac{2}{2} \geq 35$ (D) $\frac{n}{2} \geq 35$

26. Evaluate the polynomial

$$8a^2 (5a^2 - 4a + 5)$$

    (A) $40a^3 - 49a^2 + 35a$ (B) $21a^3 + 24a^2 - 6a$

    (C) $40a^4 - 32a^3 + 40a^2$ (D) $20a^2 + 48a + 64$

27. Which labeled point on the number line is closest to $\sqrt{140}$

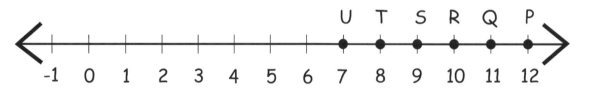

    (A) P   (B) R   (C) Q   (D) U

28. Jack has the rope of length 205.8073×10^{-2}. He needs a rope of length 2172.67×10^{-3}. How much more rope does he need to buy ?

    (A) 114.596×10^{-6} (B) 114.597×10^{-6}

    (C) 114.597×10^{-3} (D) 1145.975×10^{-3}

29. Factorize the below quadratic expression completely ?

$$3v + 9v^2$$

(A) $3v (1 - 3v^2)$ （B） $3v^2 (1 - 3v)$

(C) $3v (1 + 3v)$ （D） $v (1 + 9v)$

30. The number increased by 7 is greater than or equal to 11

(A) $r + 7 \geq 11$ （B） $11^r \geq 7$

(C) $r \times 7 >= 11$ （D） $r - 7 \geq 11$

31. A recipe for a Mexican dish needs 7 cups of rice. Ira has already put in 3 cups in the dish. How many more cups she needs to add to make the dish ?

(A) 4

(B) 6

(C) 3

(D) 5

32. Which of the below equation represents the relationship between time and book stacking (S) in the library ?

Time in minutes (T)	# of books stacked (S)
3	18
4	24
8	48
10	60
14	84

(A) $S = 6 + T$ (B) $S = 6T$ (C) $S = \dfrac{T}{6}$ (D) $S = \dfrac{6T}{T}$

33. Find the domain of the relation shown from the below data set ?

x	y
0.1	7.3
0.3	4.1
0.7	1.3
1	1.5
0.5	1.9

(A) { 7.3 , 4.1 , 1.3 , 1.5 , 1.9 }

(B) { -7.3 , 4.1 , 1.3 , -0.7 , 1 , 0.5 }

(C) { 0.11 , -0.3 , -0.7 , 1 , 0.25 }

(D) { 0.1 , 0.3 , 0.7 , 1 , 0.5 }

34. If 8 ft long iron rod of uniform thickness weighs 28 lb, what will be the weight of 10 ft long iron rod of the same thickness ?

(A)   34.8   (B)   35.9

(C)   35   (D)   36

35. Which of the below order pairs data set represents a function ?

(A) { (4 , 6) , (5.5 , 11) , (12 , 19) , (4 , 6) , (17.7 , 58) }

(B) { (4 , 6) , (5.5 , 11) , (12 , 19) , (13.2 , 31) , (12 , 58) }

(C) { (4 , 6) , (5.5 , 11) , (12 , 19) , (13.2 , 31) , (5.5 , 58) }

(D) { (4 , 6) , (5.5 , 11) , (12 , 19) , (13.2 , 31) , (17.7 , 58) }

36. Evaluate f(2), where f(x) = $2x^5 - x^2 + x$

(A) 54

(B) 62

(C) 28

(D) 42

87   www.a4ace.com   www.math-knots.com

37. What is the domain of the function y = x + 3 represented by the below graph ?

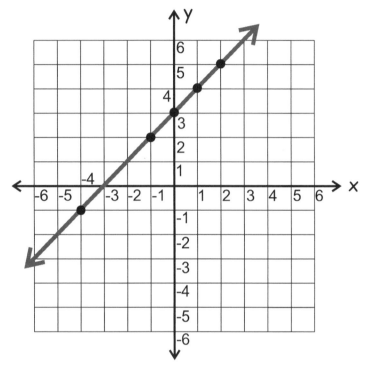

(A) D = {-4 , 0 , -1 , 1 , 2 }

(B) D = { 4 , 0 , 1 , -1 , -6 }

(C) D = {0.7 , 1 , -2.5 , 5 , -6.9 }

(D) D = {6.5 , 2 , 3.5 , - 4 , -2 }

38. What is the range of the function f(x) = x^2 - 14x -15 where Domain = { -1 , -2 , 0 , 2 , 5 }

(A) { 9 , 17 , 15 , 39 , -60 }

(B) { 17 , 17 , -15 , -39 , 60 }

(C) { 0 , -17 , -15 , -39 , 60 }

(D) { 0 , 17 , -15 , -39 , -60 }

39. Which graph best represents a direct variation ?

$$y = 3x$$

(A)

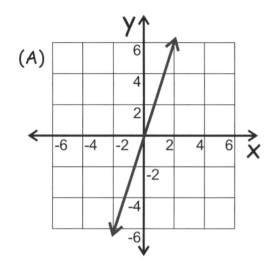

(B)

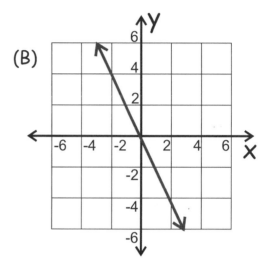

(C)

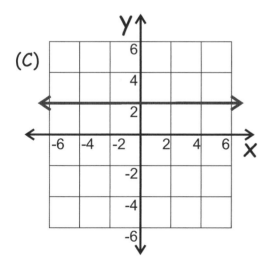

(D)

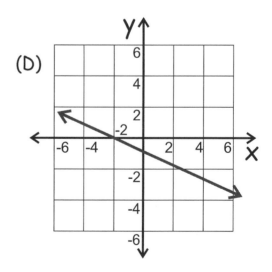

40. Which of the below tables shows the relation between X and Y as direct variation.

(A)

x	y
1	11
5	55
10	110
15	165
20	220

(B)

x	y
1	11
5	50
10	110
15	15
20	240

(C)

x	y
1	1
5	67
10	18
15	33
20	91

(D)

x	y
1	101
5	45
10	115
15	165
20	220

41. Super smooth ice-cream store sells ice cream scoop at a flat rate of $3.75 with a charge for toppings as given below.

# Ice Cream toppings (T)	Sale Price $ (P)
0	3.75
1	4.25
3	5.25
5	6.25
10	8.75

Which of the below gives the total price (C) of "T" toppings ?

(A)   C = 3.75P - 0.5T

(B)   C = 3.4P - 0.50T

(C)   C = 4.25P

(D)   C = 3.75 + 0.50T

42. Which of the below graph best represents the function

$$f(x) = x^2 - x - 2$$

(A)

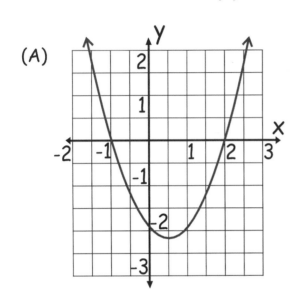

(B)

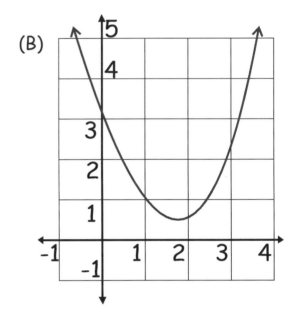

(C)

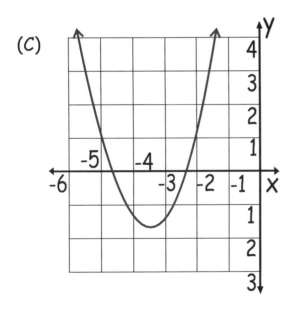

(D)

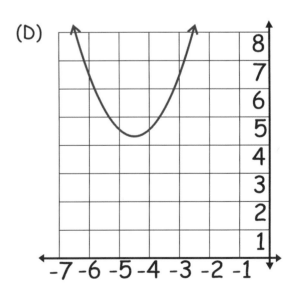

43. Find the sum of the below Matrices ?

$$
\begin{vmatrix} 3 & 5 \\ -3 & -1 \\ 7 & 2 \end{vmatrix} + \begin{vmatrix} 7 & 0 \\ -2 & 4 \\ 6 & -6 \end{vmatrix}
$$

(A) $\begin{vmatrix} 10 & 5 \\ -5 & 3 \\ 13 & -4 \end{vmatrix}$ (B) $\begin{vmatrix} 10 & 8 \\ -4 & 13 \\ 12 & 5 \end{vmatrix}$

(C) $\begin{vmatrix} 5 & 7 \\ -7 & 8 \\ 10 & 6 \end{vmatrix}$ (D) $\begin{vmatrix} 15 & 10 \\ -10 & 6 \\ 26 & -8 \end{vmatrix}$

44. The table below shows the number of bracelets made by each class of Zara elementary school for a fund raiser sales that is upcoming

Bracelets made by 6th grade school

Day	Class#1	Class#2	Class#3	Class#4
Monday	101	119	121	301
Tuesday	302	210	435	199
Wednesday	170	431	295	398
Thursday	220	75	750	452
Friday	310	190	660	595

Which sixth grade class made the highest number of bracelets for the fundraiser ?

(A) Class # 2

(B) Class # 1

(C) Class# 3

(D) Class # 4

45. Which equation is the line of best fit for the data in the below table?

x	y
0	7
2	3
6	-5
8	-9
9	-11

(A) Y = -2X + 1

(B) Y = -2X + 7

(C) Y = -2X + 5

(D) Y = 2X + 1

46. Which graph best represents the below data ?

Chess tournament 2019

Team Name	Score	Team Name	Score
Bishop Brigades	28	The chessmates	4
The Square pears	1	check matie	7
Rolling Pawns	2	Catholic	1
Rook and Roll	5	Petrojan Horse	1
Chess for life	28	Nevada	6
White knights	25	Kings of the 64	1
Pawn Shop	9	Soldiers	37
Black & White	3		
The knight mates	5		
Board lords	9		
Chess nuts	4		
Unruly Queens	26		
Magnus	4		
Wild Horses	9		

(A)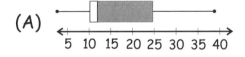

(B)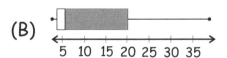

(C)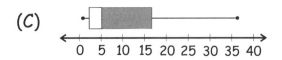

(D)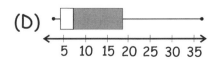

47. Which is most likely the best fit for the below equation ?

$$y = -5x + 3$$

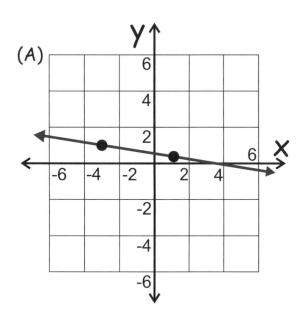

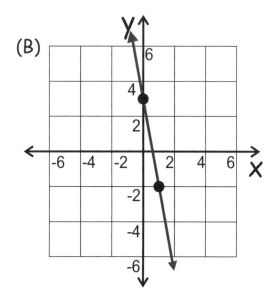

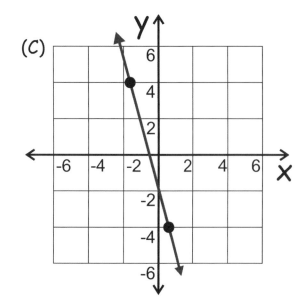

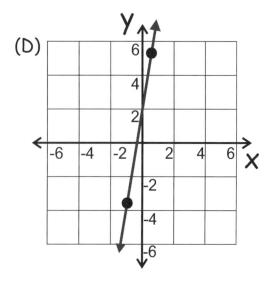

48. Rik solved below number of math problems each week

    69, 53, 61, 16, 33, 62

    He then solved 58 more after the week . How are the mean and median affected ?

    (A) The mean and the median both decreased.
    (B) The median decreased and the mean is increased.
    (C) The median and the mean both remained the same.
    (D) The mean increased and the median increased.

49. Rock and Roll theme park charges a flat rate of $6 plus a price based on the purchaser age.

    The table below shows various ages and their associated prices.

Age	Cost ($)	Item Name	Cost ($)
7 - 10	5	19 - 22	12
11 - 14	7	23 - 26	15
15 - 18	9	27 - 30	15

    If twenty people in each age group came to the theme park today. Which of the below represents the total money collected ?

    (A) $120 \begin{vmatrix} 5 & 12 \\ 7 & 15 \\ 9 & 15 \end{vmatrix}$

    (B) $14 \begin{vmatrix} 55 & 32 \\ 48 & 41 \\ 63 & 59 \end{vmatrix}$

    (C) $7 \begin{vmatrix} 55 & 32 \\ 48 & 41 \\ 63 & 59 \end{vmatrix}$

    (D) $18 \begin{vmatrix} 25 & 55 \\ 11 & 47 \\ 38 & 35 \end{vmatrix}$

www.a4ace.com   www.math-knots.com

50. Add and evaluate the below

$$\begin{vmatrix} 1 & 6 \\ 15 & 5 \\ 3 & 4 \end{vmatrix} \quad + \quad \begin{vmatrix} 10 & -8 \\ -7 & -12 \\ 11 & 9 \end{vmatrix} \quad = \quad ?$$

(A) $\begin{vmatrix} 11 & -2 \\ 8 & -7 \\ 14 & 13 \end{vmatrix}$

(B) $\begin{vmatrix} -15 & 10 \\ 7 & 8 \\ 17 & -5 \end{vmatrix}$

(C) $\begin{vmatrix} 1 & 2 \\ 0 & -9 \\ 9 & 10 \end{vmatrix}$

(D) $\begin{vmatrix} 4 & 1 \\ 7 & -7 \\ 5 & 6 \end{vmatrix}$

ALGEBRA 1
SOL
Practice Test - 1
Answer Keys

www.a4ace.com   www.math-knots.com

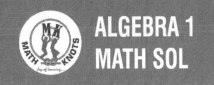
Answer Key Test - 1

1. B

2. B

3. C

4. A

5. D

6. B

7. C

8. A

9. C

10. A

11. C

12. A

13. D

14. A

15. C

16. D

17. B

18. D

19. D

20. B

21. D

22. C

23. A

24. B

25. A

26. C

27. C

28. A

29. D

30. B

31. C

32. A

33. A

34. B

35. C

36. A

37. A

38. A

39. A

40. C

41. A

42. D

43. B

44. C

45. A

46. D

 www.a4ace.com   www.math-knots.com

47. D

48. A

49. C

50. B

ALGEBRA 1
SOL
Practice Test - 2
Answer Keys

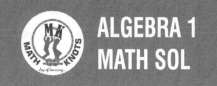
<u>Answer Key Test - 2</u>

1. D

2. D

3. C

4. D

5. B

6. B

7. A

8. C

9. D

10. D

11. B

12. C

13. A

14. D

15. C

16.   B

17.   D

18.   A

19.   D

20.   C

21.   A

22.   D

23.   D

24.   C

25.   A

26.   D

27.   B

28.   C

29.   D

30.   B

31. D

32. D

33. C

34. B

35. C

36. D

37. A

38. C

39. A

40. A

41. C

42. B

43. A

44. C

45. D

46. D

47.   B

48.   B

49.   A

50.   A

ALGEBRA 1
SOL
Practice Test - 3
Answer Keys

www.a4ace.com

www.math-knots.com

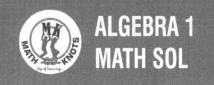

Answer Key Test - 3

1.   A

2.   D

3.   C

4.   B

5.   D

6.   C

7.   A

8.   C

9.   B

10.   A

11.   B

12.   A

13.   D

14.   B

15.   D

16. A

17. A

18. C

19. A

20. D

21. C

22. A

23. B

24. B

25. D

26. C

27. A

28. C

29. C

30. A

31. A

32. B

33. D

34. C

35. D

36. B

37. A

38. D

39. A

40. A

41. D

42. A

43. A

44. C

45. B

46. C

115   www.a4ace.com   www.math-knots.com

47. B

48. D

49. A

50. A

Algebra 1 Score calculation

If you get this many times correct :	Then your converted scale scor is :
0	000
1	217
2	249
3	268
4	282
5	293
6	303
7	311
8	319
9	325
10	331
11	337
12	343
13	348
14	353
15	357
16	362
17	366
18	371
19	375

20	379
21	383
22	387
23	391
24	395
25	399
26	403
27	407
28	411
29	415
30	419
31	423
32	427
33	432
34	436
35	441
36	445
37	450
38	456
39	461

40	467
41	473
42	480
43	487
44	496
45	505
46	516
47	531
48	550
49	582
50	600

121   www.a4ace.com   www.math-knots.com

Made in the USA
Middletown, DE
08 May 2022